Bath Farmers' Market

A case study

Farmers' Markets - An American Success Story
Harriet Festing

With over 1 million people visiting farmers' markets every week they are a definite success story. The author has spent five years researching and documenting this phenomenon. By providing facts, figures and numerous case studies, the book helps answer many questions raised about repeating their success in the UK.

Farmers' Markets - The UK Potential
Alan Chubb

By drawing on experience from Europe and other countries and concentrating on the current state of ordinary markets in the UK, this book investigates the potential benefits that farmers' markets can bring to a locality. By considering potential problems and important criteria it helps gauge the potential for the success of a particular project.

The above books can be ordered from éco-logic books. For more information and a free mail order catalogue of books that promote practical solutions to environmental problems, send an s.a.e. to:

éco-logic books
Mulberry House, 19 Maple Grove
Bath BA2 3AF, England
Tel 01225 484472
Fax 0117 942 0164

Bath Farmers' Market

A case study

Edited by Pat Tutt and Deborah Morris

Research by Alan Chubb

éco-logic **books**

Further information on the Bath Farmers' Market can be obtained from:

**Pat Tutt (01 225) 477653 or
Deborah Morris (01 225) 477662,
Agenda 21 Unit,
Bath and North East Somerset District Council,
Trim Street, Bath BA1 2DP**

First published in 1998 by éco-logic books

éco-logic books is an imprint of Worldly Goods

Worldly Goods publishes and distributes books that promote practical solutions to environmental and social problems.
For further information contact:

Worldly Goods
10-12 Picton Street
Bristol BS6 5QA

ISBN 1 899233 03 2

Photographs   Carlo Chinca
Design and typesetting   Jon Carpenter
Cover design   Helen Miller Designs
Printing and binding   Doveton Press, Bristol

Contents

Acknowledgements

Setting up the Bath Farmers' Market was an immense challenge for the organisers and the producers alike. Together, they made the U.K.'s first farmers' market a success. The Bath Farmers' Market is a true example of partnership working towards sustainable development.

The project was managed by members of a working group from the public, private and voluntary sectors and was made possible by their determination and commitment. The members were;

Poppy Hayward, Bath Environment Centre

Peter Andrews, Bath Permaculture Trust and publisher

Tim Baines, Bath Organic Group and landscape gardener

Pat Tutt, LA 21 Coordinator, Bath and North East Somerset Council

Deborah Morris, Assistant LA 21 Officer, Bath and North East Somerset Council

Christian Taylor, Eco Futures Group and university student

Sarah May, Bath Farmers' Market Project Officer and smallholder

Alan Chubb, Bath Farmers' Market Reporting Officer and horticulturist

Thanks go to all of them for holding on to their shared vision of a Bath Farmers' Market and for the many hours of time they put towards making the project a success. Thanks go to the producers who take such pride in growing and selling their produce. Thanks also to Harriet Festing of Wye College of Agriculture for stirring us to action with her written and spoken words and to Cathy Thompson who planted the first seed of the idea and tended its early shoots.

The Bath Farmers' Market project was made possible by funding and support from Bath and North East Somerset Council.

Foreword

Farmers' Markets could and should thrive throughout Britain. The country has a history of small-scale, local markets selling local produce to local people. The skills and knowledge needed for a farmers' market still exist within communities: small-scale farmers are selling good quality produce through farm shops and other local outlets; voluntary groups are promoting organic growing, allotments and local food production; local authorities are working to strengthen local economies and the local environment; and consumers are keen to buy direct from the producer in order that they can get first hand knowledge of the quality and safety of their food. The purpose of this case study is to encourage these groups to work together in partnership.

We believe the Bath Farmers' Market project was a success for two reasons. First, the project adhered to the vision of a local market with local produce sold by local producers and used and enjoyed by local people. Strict criteria, based on the principles of sustainable development, were set and referred to throughout the project. Second, the project was achieved through a strong partnership made up of the public, private and voluntary sectors, each bringing with them their skills and resources.

The organisers hope that the framework presented here will be of assistance and encouragement to others wishing to set up a farmers' market in their area.

The Bath Farmers' Market Working Group

local produce for local people
at the

FARMERS' MARKET
BATH

Green Park Station

9.30 a.m. until 3.30 p.m.

Saturday

27 September • 18 October • 15 November

Coverage by the **BBC** *Food Programme*

Quality • Freshness • Locally produced • Organic • Free-range • Wholefood
• *Live Entertainment Fun & Festivities* •

1 What is a farmers' market?

The concept of farmers' markets is not a new one. Farmers have bartered and sold goods as far back in history as agriculture itself. The term 'farmers' market' is used here in a very specific way. It is based on the model of a type of market currently on the increase in the USA and which is very different in nature to the kind of street markets which have become familiar in Britain. Simply, a farmers' market sells locally produced goods to local people. No goods are sold by middlemen and no goods are imported from outside the area. So, local goods for local people.

Bath Farmers' Market, September 1997.

Farmers' markets and Local Agenda 21

Local Agenda 21 has been adopted by over 70% of local authorities and their communities in the U.K. It came from an international agreement reached at the United Nations Earth Summit in Rio in 1992. The agreement calls on communities to develop and implement a local plan for improving the quality of life in their areas into the 21st century (a Local Agenda 21).

The production, distribution and consumption of food offers many opportunities for addressing quality of life issues including environmental, economic and social concerns. Farmers' markets are one such opportunity. The main emphasis of these markets is that they help local producers to sell their goods near their source of origin, creating benefits to them and to the local community. They benefit the local economy by keeping money circulating within the community, encouraging agricultural diversification, and attracting people to adjacent retail businesses. They benefit the local environment by encouraging small-scale less intensive production, reducing the effects of long distance transport of food, and reduced packaging. They benefit producers and consumers by providing a social meeting point, giving them direct contact with each other, and encouraging goodwill and understanding

Farmers' Markets benefit producers and consumers alike.

between rural and urban populations. The information sheet in the press pack (Appendix 5) outlines these benefits in greater detail.

Aims and objectives of the Bath Farmers' Market project

Aim:

To create a vibrant, self sustaining Farmers' Market in Bath based on the principles of sustainable development .

Objectives:

- To set up three 'pilot' Farmers' Markets in Bath
- To assess the commercial viability of a Farmers' Market in Bath after the pilot project
- To measure and monitor the three 'pilot' markets
- To report and share good practice on the experience gained by the project
- To assess what future support the Farmers' Market requires in order to continue and to assist with that support wherever possible

Background to the Bath Farmers' Market

Four separate strands came together to bring about the Farmers' Market project in Bath:

a. Recommendations of the B&NES Local Agenda 21 Issue Commission

Bath and North East Somerset Council (B&NES) had agreed to encourage the production and consumption of local food as a way of addressing some of the social, economic and environmental problems which concerned local people.

Evidence of peoples' concerns had been gathered by a Local Agenda 21 Issue Commission, set up by the Council to recommend ways in which key concerns effecting quality of life in the region could be addressed through the Local Agenda 21 process.

b. Award funding

B&NES Council won an award of £2,000 from 'Label 21', an award scheme sponsored by the National Westminster Bank. Judges for the scheme liked the proposal for a local food links project to enhance local food production and supply, submitted by the Local Agenda 21 Co-ordinator.

"Issues had been identified; a process to address these issues was in place; money was available. We needed to develop the project further."

c. Harriet's article

The Council's Local Agenda 21 Co-ordinator saw an article about farmers' markets in the journal of the Town and Country Planning Association. The author was Harriet Festing of the University of London at Wye College, Kent. Harriet had done research on farmers' markets in the U.S. and was working to promote the concept in Britain. She was invited to come to Bath in February 1997 to give a presentation. Among those invited were Council officers from the economic development, policy and environment sections of the authority, elected members, project officers from the Bath Environment Centre and representatives from local organic groups.

"We had found our project. To develop it we needed partners."

d. Apple Day Working Group

An existing partnership, the Apple Day Working Group, was looking for ideas for an Apple Day event in Bath. Members of the group, from the Council's Local Agenda 21 team, the Bath Environment Centre, Bath Permaculture Trust and Bath Organic Group, had planned and organised two successful festivals in previous years, but wanted a different kind of event for Apple Day '97. (Apple Day is a national calendar event to raise awareness of local distinctiveness and the value of traditional orchards and apples.) There would be festivities and street theatre, and local produce on sale. Bee-keepers, apple growers, and cider and juice makers were keen to be involved again. Their produce had sold well on previous Apple Day events.

The working group decided to have a series of markets in the city. Three markets, each with a different theme: 'Harvest', 'Apples and Orchards', and 'Christmas'. The markets would sell only local produce. Produce would be sold by the people who produced it. Street entertainment would be an essential feature. In effect, the markets would be farmers' markets.

"Our project didn't so much develop as evolve. But it wouldn't have got very far without more producers."

2 What we did

The information in this section is not presented in any specific order. It does not represent the chronological process of development for the project. As in all project development, many of these activities and processes were happening simultaneously. Nor does the presentation reflect the priority given to any of these activities. Priorities can only be identified within the specific local circumstances that any project finds itself. A chronological presentation of our activities is outlined in Appendix 1.

Funding and costs

Our market was a 'test bed' for the concept both nationally and locally. To our knowledge this was the first farmers' market in the UK. We recognised that some extra expenditure was necessary to develop a concept that had not been tried and tested in this country. Hopefully for those setting out now, armed with the information in this case study and the knowledge that it can be done, there will be less uncertainty over funding and costs. A group hoping to set up a farmers' market should be able to do so without the same developmental overheads required in this case. In the section entitled 'Costs' we have tried to identify the running costs of our market without the development costs that we experienced.

a. Funding

Our market was funded from three main sources. Funds were secured by B&NES Council through the 'Label 21' awards sponsored by the National Westminster Bank and administered by the Local Government Management Board. Supplementary funding was agreed from the Economic Development section of B&NES. The largest amount of funding came from the B&NES Local Agenda 21 budget.

Label 21 Awards (NatWest Bank)	£2,000
B&NES Economic Development	£1,750
B&NES LA21 Budget	£ 9,000

b. Costs

The second column of costs in the table below identifies what we hope will be the ongoing running costs of the market.

Item	Establishment/Capital costs for 3 markets (£)	Estimated running costs/market (£)
Staffing: 2 Project Officers (does not include considerable voluntary and local authority officer time)	8,000	160
Publicity; • Leaflet design/ printing/ distribution (20,000 for first 3 mkts)	610	(i) 158
• Banner and 'A' boards	(one off) 500	(ii)
Extra Items • Table coverings	320	(ii) 0
• Brown paper bags with logo	300	
Electrical board for refrigeration	160	
Recording the event: • Professional photography	500	0
• Video coverage	60	0
Entertainments: Jugglers	200	(iii) 0
Guitarist	75	0
Dancers	60	0
Musicians	180	0
Puppets	180	60
Others	50	0
Market decorations (seasonal)	90	50
Hiring of site	1200	350
Total	12,485	(iv) 778
Income Generated	Stall fees 750	678

(i)   Publicity/advertising — at the beginning of setting up a market these costs will be high. As the market becomes a regular activity with a regular date either once or twice a month, these costs will reduce as consumers become accustomed to the dates (i.e. the first Saturday in each month). (See also section entitled 'Publicity and Advertising')

(ii) Start-up costs — some of these could be offset over time if the stallholders were willing to absorb them.

(iii) Entertainment — the intention will be to test if the entertainment costs can be reduced through 'controlled' busking. We will try offering pitches to invited buskers to test this option. We felt that the children's entertainment was important enough to retain as a regular cost. (See section entitled 'Entertainment')

(iv) If the market is to continue on a self financing basis the stallholders must cover these costs. The costs identified here are the minimum operational costs and until the stallholders set up an 'association' to manage the market in the future. It is difficult to be certain of these estimates. These costs do not reflect the need for the market to remain innovative and retain a strong customer base.

Commercial street markets charge £2.10-£2.90/ft or £12-£17/table although these markets are not directly comparable to farmers' markets in that they attract a lower spending custom and they are usually not under cover.

The preparatory stages

a. Researching and building the producer database

The early stages of the project involved building a database of potential producers. This was achieved by following a number of approaches:

- By selecting potential producers and processors from the B&NES Environmental Health and the Trading Standards premises listings that are compiled for regulatory use by the local authority.
- The Soil Association was able to provide a list of their members. Those that fell within our working area and had appropriate produce were included.
- Groups such as the WI and Allotments Associations were contacted through local networks.
- By selecting from a local food guide entitled *Tastes of the West* which listed specialist suppliers.
- By word of mouth and personal contacts known to the Working Group members and project officers.

First contact with producers was made by way of a letter describing the proposed project and requesting the return of a slip to identify level of interest. Little interest was generated this way and it was left to the

Market Project Officer to make personal contact with as many producers as possible by telephone. Her skills were essential to convince and cajole the producers to attend the first market.

Once the aims and objectives were agreed by the Working Group it quickly became apparent that the pressure of time was upon us. Realistically the autumn months, September, October and November were the latest possible dates to run the three pilot markets. The existing budget also had to be spent before the end of the financial year in April, 1998 and the spring months were not appropriate for starting an initiative that relied on local produce.

b. Project Officer Recruitment

The Working Group drew up job descriptions for two posts: the Farmers' Market Project Officer and the Farmers' Market Research Officer (Appendix 2) and advertised the posts locally. It was also decided that it would be the responsibility of the Bath Environment Centre to provide line management and office facilities for these posts.

The Farmers' Market Project Officer was recruited for 2 days/week for a period of 5 months. The successful candidate had good practical experience in small-scale vegetable production and marketing. Realistically, the Project Officer worked up to 4 days per week as the project required far more time in the early stages. The funding was able to accommodate this.

The Reporting Officer was recruited for 1 day/week for 5 months. The successful candidate had extensive experience in horticultural production and marketing with established report writing skills

Market guidelines and rules

In order to differentiate the Bath Farmers' Market from other markets it was important to inform the potential producer/participants exactly how farmers' markets are distinct from other markets, and of their benefits to the producer. This was done by way of an information sheet. (See Appendix 5.)

Guidelines for stallholders were produced including;
- General guidelines outlining basic do's and don'ts in stocking and running their stall especially outlining the fact that only home-grown produce should be sold. (Appendix 3.)
- More specific guidelines covering the sales of fruit and vegetables

People have an opportunity to taste the produce and talk directly to the producers.

(this was included to assist those not accustomed to market selling who were expected to be mostly 'amateur' fruit and vegetable producers). (Appendix 3.)

Regulations and enforcement

'It is so nice to be working with the Council for a change.' (A stallholder)

Regulations influence many of the activities that go on in a farmers' market. The majority of the activities are regulated by the local authority although liquor licensing is the responsibility of the local magistrates court.

It is important to have the various regulatory functions of the local authority aware of and, if possible, in support of the market at the earliest possible point in the project. To facilitate this the B&NES LA 21 Coordinator drew up a list of contacts from the Council's own regulators to field any questions that the Market Project Officer or traders may have had. The LA 21 Coordinator also met with senior managers to inform them and seek their support for the project. Additionally, elected members were kept informed throughout the setting up and implementation of the market. The efforts to ensure that all of these elements of the local authority were 'on board' proved worthwhile in overcoming any potential for confusion and uncertainty during the setting up of the market.

The following is a list of the enforcement agencies that were contacted as part of the Bath project. The list identifies the regulatory activities and also gives a note on how these related to the Bath Market.

a. Bath and North East Somerset Council Unitary Authority

Please note — these functions may be divided between a District and County Council in an area where there are two tiers of local government.

Planning section: planning permission is required for a permanent market and may be required for a temporary market. If the market is held in a listed building, consent will be required for any alterations to the building and for advertising.

The Bath Farmers' Market was held on an existing market site that already had planning permission to operate.

Environmental Health section: anyone operating as a food business must seek registration and undergo food hygiene inspections of their premises. There are strict controls over temperatures for hot and cold foods that must be observed during storage, during transportation to the market, and during the operations of the market itself.

The Bath Farmers' Market found that most of its participating producers were fully aware of the food hygiene regulations as they had been selling at other markets (i.e. WI Markets) or from their own farm shops. Refrigeration was required for many foods (e.g. meat and dairy products), although most traders supplied their own chilled storage. Environmental Health Officers were encouraged to attend the markets and made useful comments about compliance to the B&NES LA 21 Co-ordinator.

Trading Standards section: Trading standards Officers check the accuracy and suitability of weighing and measuring equipment, and that goods sold to the public are the correct weight. They check that food is marked and priced according to legal requirements. They also check safety and labelling requirements for non-food items.

The Bath Farmers' Market found that most of its 'commercial' producers were well aware of the requirements for weights and labelling. The 'non-commercial' groups (i.e. allotment holders) were asked to weigh and label before the event if they did not have access to scales. The WI have well established routines for both food safety and trading standards. An informal visit to the site by a Trading Standards Officer did not raise immediate concerns and the officer will be returning for a formal inspection in the near future.

Highways section: Highways Officers deal with the regulations and processing involved in street closures and highway signage.

The Bath Farmers' Market did not require a road closure and liaison was undertaken with the Highways section when we considered using AA or RAC signage. In the event, these were not used.

Licensing section: Licensing officers issue licences for entertainments and events as well as street trading. Busking in Bath is managed through a voluntary 'code of practice' and noise complaints that result from inappropriate busking are dealt with by Environmental Health Officers.

The Bath Farmers' Market did not require any licensing as entertainment was deemed 'secondary' to the purpose of the market. It did not require street trading permits as it was on a permitted market site.

b. Other enforcement agencies

Magistrates' Court. Liquor licensing is managed by the Magistrates' Court and enforced by the police.

The Bath Farmers' Market found this a time-consuming and complicated undertaking, perhaps as the agency was not in regular contact with any of the organisers, unlike the regulators within the council. Application was made by one of the full on-licence holders and the intention was to cover the other liquor sellers through this licence. There was considerable confusion over this and the police did agree to come to the market to ensure that sales were being undertaken according to their requirements. Duly, a police officer did attend and was happy with the arrangements.

Fire Department: All fire regulations with respect to an event and/or building are enforced by the Fire Department.

The Bath Farmers' Market did liaise with the fire officer at the request of Green Park Station management to ensure that all regulations were being followed. The Fire Officer's comments proved useful with respect to fire extinguishers and ensuring fire exits were kept clear.

c. Other considerations

Insurance: It was advised that all sellers should have a public liability insurance. Those with farm shops or who sold at other markets had this cover already. As the market took place on premises where a market was already operating, this insurance was in fact already in place for participating stallholders. The Market Project Officer also required Professional Indemnity Insurance but as this would have cost £500/year. To overcome this, the Bath Environment Centre included this cover under their own insurance for the duration of the pilot project.

Selection of producers

The Working Group had discussed and decided on two criteria that would influence the selection of producers; the distance from the market and the need for direct selling by the producer. Both of these criteria fit well with the core principles of the project. By adhering to these two criteria some elements of the selection process were in place. The need to ensure that a variety of produce was available was also recognised. The role of the Market Project Officer was to prove crucial in the management of the selection process.

Distance from the market. Many concerns could be addressed by setting a reasonably local limit to the distance that the stallholders would travel. Food miles would be kept to a minimum, consumers could readily access the farmer/stallholder when the market was not running and the positive effect on the local economy would be greater. The Working Group decided on a limit of a 40 mile radius around Bath as an initial recruiting area. If insufficient numbers of willing producers were not located the area could be expanded if necessary. This was found to be not necessary.

Direct selling by producers. Direct selling would ensure that the producer/consumer relationship was allowed to develop. Only producers themselves, their immediate family or employee would be allowed to sell at the market. The selling of other farmers' produce would not be allowed except in the cases of not-for-profit, co-operative marketing groups such as the WI, The Bath Organic Group and the Bath Allotments Association.

The need for a variety of produce. The Working Group felt that it was important to get as wide a range of produce for sale as possible to keep the consumers interested. Thus it was necessary to have a number of sellers from each category of produce.

The Market Project Officer took on this difficult task and performed it admirably. The issues of competition between stallholders with the same type of produce (e.g. fruit and veg) was discussed and we felt that this was not an issue we could address until an association of producers was formed. The skills of the project officer came into play and her assertiveness, tact, diplomacy and courage were all a great asset. The pilot markets all ended up with a good balance of producers. (See table below.)

Category of produce	1st market	2nd market	3rd market
dairy produce	3	3	3
meat	3	2	5
fruit and vegetables	7	9	9
smoked meat	1	1	1
preserves	1	2	1
baked goods	2	1	2
fruit juice/cider/wine	4	2	4
crafts	2	2	2
honey	1	1	1
plants/herbs	2	2	2
other	0	2	6
Total	**26**	**27**	**36**

Below and opposite: Fruit and vegetables, cheese, cider and apple juice …
and local ostrich pie!

POTENTIAL SITE	LOCATION	WEATHER PROTECTION	AVAILABILITY	ACCESS	COMMENTS
Green Park Station	• not in centre of Bath but close to suburbs • beside large supermarket	• attractive glass roof over old train station site	• largely under-used	• trader unloading alongside • good public access	• attractive site • close to Sainsbury's • parking for traders a problem • existing market on site
Twerton Street Market	• in suburb of Bath	• open air	• restricted on weekends	• trader unloading alongside • good public access	• in the car park of a football ground • not attractive • existing market on site
Walcot flea and antique market	• close to centre of Bath	• covered • site in need of repair	• not available Saturdays	• trader unloading alongside • good public access	• well located and known by the public
Abbey Churchyard	• centre of Bath • popular tourist area	• open air	• council owned	• trader unloading alongside • good public access	• well popu-lated area • no nearby trader parking
Bath Street	• centre of Bath • popular tourist area	• open air	• possible	• trader unloading alongside • good public access	• attractive site • considerable current building work • no nearby trader parking
The Pavilion	• near centre of Bath	• covered	• restricted on Sundays	• trader unloading alongside • good public access	• expensive to hire
York Street and Abbeygate Street	• near centre of Bath	• open air	• possible	• trader unloading alongside • good public access	• attractive cobbled back streets • needing closure orders • no nearby trader parking
Broad St & Walcott St council-owned car parks	• centre of Bath	• open air	• possible	• trader unloading alongside • good public access	• not attractive locations • required to reimburse council for lost parking fees
Queens Square	• centre of Bath	• open air	• possible	• trader unloading alongside • difficult access due to roads	• attractive small park with grass and trees • poor access • surrounded by busy roads on four sides

The site assessment exercise

Site selection

Criteria for site selection were discussed and the following considered the most important:

Accessibility — it was important that the site had good access for traders. They needed to get their goods close to the site and have limited obstacles for their unloading. It was also important that the site be as accessible as possible for the consumers including the elderly, children and disabled people.

Weather Protection — as the markets would be taking place during the autumn, cover was felt to be an important consideration. We could not source reasonably priced covered stalls and so the site had to be covered or able to take a marquee.

Site Rental — with a limited budget site rental costs were a consideration.

Location — was felt to be an important consideration as it was felt that considerable publicity would be required for any site that was out of the main city centre shopping precinct.

Other — on sites with existing markets it was felt important that the Farmers' Market would have to be clearly differentiated from the other

A listed Victorian railway station provided a very good site for the Bath Farmers' Markets

operations. The availability of nearby parking for traders was also a concern.

A total of 13 potential sites were identified and considered. Each had its own strengths and weaknesses.

a. Site assessment exercise (see page 16).

b. Our choice

The Green Park Station site was finally selected because;
* it was covered and had electric and water for stallholders
* it had public toilet facilities
* it had an existing planning permission to operate as a market
* the cost of the site was reasonable
* it had enough space to accommodate in excess of 30 producers
* it had reasonably close parking for traders
* it had good access for trader unloading and good customer accessibility

Our concerns for the site were;
* being out of the city centre it would require considerable publicity and advertising
* there was a small existing market on the site on Saturdays and our market would require differentiation
* there was some potential for conflict with surrounding traders and a supermarket. We wanted to minimise this

Publicity and advertising

"Given the current groundswell of concern about food issues, we felt sure that our Farmers' Market experiment was ripe for media attention — and 'photogenic' to boot."

Since our first market in September we have enjoyed a lot of attention from the national media. In this respect our publicity campaign was a stunning success. Our project was featured on BBC television's 'Country File' and 'The Really Useful Show'; and BBC Radio 4's early morning 'Farming Today'. It got onto The Back Page of *The Independent*, and into several newsletters, specialist journals and glossy 'lifestyle' magazines.

Timing and preparation were crucial to this success, but also significant were certain coincidences: much stemmed from our contact with Henrietta Green, food writer and broadcaster for BBC Radio 4's 'The

Food Programme'. Getting on 'The Food Programme' was the real coup.

We got in touch with Henrietta through The Food Writers' Guild about a month before our first market. At the time, she happened to be writing a piece about farmers' markets for *Country Living*, having recently been to the USA. Also, 'The Food Programme' team were working on the first programme in a new series. This happened to share the same 'Harvest' theme of our first Farmers' Market.

"We knew we had a 'hit' when the phones started ringing immediately after The Food Programme broadcast."

We were delighted with the programme. The programme makers were pleased about our markets — they provided good news and a happy conclusion to their first programme. Many people all over the country were inspired. We know this because they have called and written to tell us. In a 'colourful', entertaining and informative way, 'The Food Programme' captured perfectly the essence of what our publicity campaign was striving to achieve, which was:

1. To advertise the markets, for maximum attendance.
2. To explain and promote the distinctive characteristics and the benefits of farmers' markets.
3. To raise awareness of the social, economic and environmental issues pertinent to the Bath Farmers' Market project.
4. To raise the profile of, and explain the Local Agenda 21 process, using the markets as tangible examples of Local Agenda 21 happening 'on the ground'.

Broadly, our publicity campaign had three elements: advertising, education and public relations. Research undertaken at all three markets identified radio and television as the consumers' main source of information (see Appendix 8).

a. Advertising

We gave our project an identity by designing a logo. Our logo was used in all of our advertising, and also stamped onto brown paper carrier bags, issued to stallholders to give to shoppers.

We advertised the markets in the following ways:

Flyers

We designed a flyer and had several thousand printed. These were left in doctors' surgeries, libraries, tourist information points, shops, Council reception areas, and distributed door to door through the local free newspapers. (Appendix 4.)

'What's On' guides and slots on local television and radio

The *What's On in Bath* guide gave us free listings. In addition we placed a quarter page advertisement in *Venue* magazine. The front of our flyer worked very well for the advertisement.

News of the markets as forthcoming events was also given air time on regional television programmes such as 'What's on in the West', and broadcast by several local radio stations.

Banner

Our banner served three purposes: it advertised each market over the full week leading up to each event; it attracted people using the adjacent car park; and it helped to distinguish the markets — people could see these were farmers' markets and not any other sort. Also, we thought it looked quite good on television!

A boards

We had two A boards made, with the intention of putting one outside Green Park Station and the other in the city centre. However one very quickly went missing. Perhaps we should not have asked for it to have a handle for ease of carriage! Another useful feature of the A boards was a blackboard insert, to allow dates and times to be changed.

The local press

News releases were mailed out to all regional newspapers in Bath and North East Somerset. Releases were written up before and after each event. Each release took a different angle, for example: The first served to introduce the project and the players; the second reported on the event from a producer angle (glowing quotations from shoppers, stall-holders and nearby tradespeople were very useful here — Appendix 5), and offered photo opportunities for the press to get pictures and inter-views of the producers; the third news release talked about the project's success in terms of the national attention it was attracting, and the impli-cations of this for shopping patterns nationwide. And so on. New angles presented themselves regularly as the project developed, providing news that was suitable for a variety of different columns in the newspapers. For example, *The Bath Chronicle* gave coverage of the markets in their

'Agenda', 'What's On', 'Bath News' and 'Your Letters' pages, depending on the angle of news supplied.

Incidentally, a rather grumpy letter to *The Bath Chronicle*, complaining about perceived traffic problems the markets might generate, provided us with an opportunity to get more coverage by way of a positive reply.

Local radio

News releases were also sent to local radio stations, and resulted in numerous interviews over the phone.

b. Education

Advertising at Green Park Station

Flyers

Information about farmers' markets was presented as a 'Case for Farmers' Markets' on the back of the flyer (Appendix 4).

Press packs

News releases were sent out with background information: information about farmers' markets; information about Local Agenda 21; and an explanation of how the two related. This information had been prepared at the outset of the project. It was easily reproduced, and 'packaged' up ready to go. This enabled us to respond efficiently to enquiries from the media. We called these information packages 'press packs' and sent them to radio and television as well as the newspapers (Appendix 5). Packs contained:

- a news release

- a Farmers' Markets Information Sheet
- quotations from stallholders and shoppers
- a flyer (Appendix 4)

c. Public relations

We invited the Editor of our local paper, *The Bath Chronicle*, to judge the 'Best Dressed Stall' at our first market in September. Being keen on community issues, he was pleased to oblige, and since the nub of the project was 'local produce for local people — meeting local needs locally', we felt that someone from our local paper was a highly appropriate choice for this!

The public relations generated by the project have been very positive. Hundreds of letters and telephone calls to the editor of the local paper, to the Council, the Bath Environment Centre and the local Chamber of Commerce have demonstrated popular support for the project and its organisers.

Entertainment

Entertainment is an important element of a farmer's markets and helps to distinguish it from a regular street market by creating a festive atmosphere. Themed markets are an important way of keeping the farmers'

'The Mopheads'

'Bath Puppet Theatre'

market as a place of innovation and local distinctiveness, e.g. Apple Day. Market entertainment can be directly linked to local festivals or celebrations. Carol singers during a pre Christmas markets or Morris dancers at a spring market are other examples. Farmers' markets could also act as a showcase for new, emerging local talent.

Our market took the opportunity to try various sorts of entertainers and to manage their attendance by offering direct payment. This proved expensive but valuable lessons were learned on the type of entertainment preferred by customers and stallholders. Busking was not tried although would present a cost effective alternative to paid entertainers. This will be trialled at future markets when controlled busking spaces will be offered to invited performers.

Our market tried:

* Music — Instrumental folk music (mandolin and bass) was popular although a classical guitarist who attended was not as it was not loud enough. One group of enthusiastic samba players were far too loud and made trade difficult. Amplification of any music was not allowed due to concerns about noise disturbance in surrounding residential areas and the restricted nature of the site.
* Children's entertainment — we felt children's entertainment was an essential element of the market. A puppet theatre was a success as the

children were seated allowing parents to continue shopping. Jugglers and clowns who moved amongst the crowd were also popular.

- Cookery demonstrations — Local chefs were invited to prepare a meal using food available from the market. This was expensive as it required equipment rental and involved a lot of organisation but attracted customers. The smells of cooking added to the general atmosphere.

- Dancers — Clog dancers added to the occasion but meant that people stopped to watch and blocked the aisles. They also took over a relatively large area.

- Charity fund raising — We felt that this was an important element of the market to allow local charities a space to raise funds for their work. We held an auction to which stallholders donated a number of items. We held a tombola, again of items donated by stallholders. On Apple Day, a local charity raised funds by running a series of children's' activities including apple games. The charitable element of the market involved a lot of organisation for the Project Officer but created a goodwill towards the market with consumers. In the future, local charities would be encouraged to take over more of the organisation of the fund raising element themselves.

Proprietor of 'The Fish Market' cooks for the crowds.

Unloading, access and parking for traders are important considerations.

Bath Organic Group presses people's windfall apples.

Other organisational considerations

- Site plan and stall layout — Once all producers were identified an accurate site plan with allocated stall sites was drawn up. The layout needed to allow space for produce storage and public access between stalls. Stalls selling similar produce were grouped together.
- Trader unloading and parking — access to the market site had to be arranged for unloading and parking for stallholders found. This has proved difficult in Bath.
- Chilled units were required by some producers and some units were arranged for the duration of the pilot markets. Storage and delivery of these large units required a considerable amount of organisation. Assistance from Marks and Spencer plc was greatly appreciated. In the future, traders will take responsibility for their own units. The site had good access to electricity and water.
- Site decorations — As each market had a theme and decorations had to be thought out, purchased and arranged. This consisted of straw bales and wheat sheaves or hop runners that were attached to railings and pillars in and around the market. The Christmas market had a tree and seasonal decorations.
- Leaflets — most were distributed to households by a commercial company but voluntary labour was used to distribute to local businesses.
- Interviews — As part of the advertising campaign a number of television, radio and press interviews were given both before and during the markets. (see also 'Publicity and Advertising')

Surveys of the market

"Fantastic! We were selling before we unpacked the stuff this morning"
(A stallholder)

As part of the monitoring and evaluation of the markets a number of surveys and structured interviews were carried out by the Research Officer, with assistance from volunteers. Two were conducted with the producers and one was conducted with consumers. In addition, statistics were gathered on the number of people attending each of the pilot markets.

a. Producers' questionnaire

A questionnaire was sent out to all producers who had accepted the invitation to come and sell at the first farmers' market (Appendix 6). This questionnaire went out before any of them had direct experience of selling at a farmers' market. Twenty-three returns were received and analysed.

The findings were:

- Most producers were new to the business with just under half operating for less than 5 years.
- The producers had a good range of alternative sales outlets with just over half selling their produce in local shops. 40% sold through farm shops or directly to the wholesale markets although 30% still relied on local word-of-mouth sales.
- A half of the producers sold their produce at an outlet once a week and half sold produce 6-7 days a week.
- The part time and full time nature of the participating producers was reflected in the turnover expected from the market. Half of those that answered the question required £150-250 turnover whereas a quarter would be happy with £50-150. As a reflection on the success of the market 41% achieved a turnover of over £250 in the first two markets.
- The most popular time for the operation of the market was from 9.00am-4.00pm.
- 87% of the producers wanted the market to operate on Saturday.
- 50% wanted the market to operate monthly. Only 5 producers wished to sell weekly.
- 70% wanted the market to operate year round and those that didn't wished the market to continue from April to October. Just over half said they would be prepared to adjust their production plan to meet the demands of the market.
- The producers were equally divided as to whether they would supply other similar markets in the area.
- Most producers came to the market to expand their sales outlets (83%) and to take the opportunity to meet their customers. Just over half wished to participate in direct selling to the consumer.
- When asked about the future of the Farmers Market 78% wished that the market continued where only local food is sold.

Reported turnovers by individual sellers

category of produce	turnover/seller at 1st market (no. sellers)	turnover/seller at 2nd market (no. sellers)	turnover/seller at 3rd market (no. sellers)	average turnover/category
dairy	£370 (3)	£450 (3) £100	(3)	£306
honey	£100 (1)	£200 (1)	(1)	£150
herbs/plants	£100 (2)	£200 (2)	£154 (2)	£151
chutneys/preserves/baked goods	£200 (2)	£400 (3)	£300 (3) £700	£400
meat/smoked	£300 (3)	£850 (3) £550	£500 (5) £600 £700	£583
wine/beer	£250 (3)	£300 (4) £300 £400	225 (2)	£295
Vegetables	£400 (7) £180 £280 £350 £20	£500 (9) £350 £480 £380 £400 £285 £142 £30 £80	£430 (12) £220 £120 £450	£299
total adjusted for missing data	£5082	£ 8705	£8332	

b. *Producer questionnaire/telephone survey*

As a follow up exercise stallholders were telephoned immediately after the second market to get their views on the organisation of the market, their problems and their suggestions on improvements. See Appendix 7 for a copy of questionnaire. In addition details of their turnover on the day were obtained although this did not prove to be a popular request and some producers were not comfortable releasing this information. (See table above.)

The findings were:

- 11 producers who had other outlets said the market was better than their other outlets. Only 4 reported that the market was either the same or worse than their other outlets.
- 10 out of 14 producers said they had parking problems on the day and 7 out 14 said they came with insufficient stock. There was no general recommendation to improve the organisation of the market

other than improved parking for the producers, shorter opening hours, more space for the existing stalls plus a need to increase the size of the market.

c. Customer survey

A survey of customers at all three markets was carried out. A total of 197 questionnaires were completed. The surveys were conducted by 8 different volunteers over the 3 markets. Interviewers stood at both exits to the market area. People were questioned as they left the market. No selection criteria were employed to determine who should be interviewed (i.e. every tenth person). This could have led to a distortion. In most cases it was only those who had actually bought something that were interviewed. Younger persons who were interested in the event but didn't buy anything were omitted from the survey. (Age distribution data indicates this.)

An overview of the findings (complete results are in Appendix 8):

- The predominance of older people and 67% being female should influence the targeting of adverts and leaflet distribution as well as the entertainment.
- The response to the BBC Radio 4 'The Food Programme' was noticeable and the role of national and local TV and Radio coverage cannot be overstated. However newspaper articles leafleting and word-of-mouth were equally important in getting the word out.
- People are mainly attracted to the market for the fruit and vegetables because they are fresh and good quality and are being sold directly by the producer.
- 61% spent less than £10 at the market which will suggests that there is a restriction in the potential sales of high value produce.
- 75% of customers bought items a the market because they were sold directly by the producers or they liked to support local business.
- Most people wanted the market to operate weekly but most producers preferred monthly.
- The majority of customers were local with 57% travelling less than 3 miles.

d. Number of people attending

Every hour the number of people entering the market over a period of 5 minutes were counted (children excluded). This was carried out at

2 points of the market so that all those entering could be seen. A total of 6 counts were completed (each hour for 6 hours that the market continued). Thus it was possible to calculate the total number of potential customers.

The findings:

	1st market	2nd market	3rd market
Numbers attending	3720	5200	5196

Comments on the findings

The success of the market was reflected in the large turnout recorded. A study of the hourly flow of people shows a peak at 11 to 12 o'clock with about half of the customers visiting during this period. This meant that the aisles were too crowded for comfort and some customers reported problems especially those with children.

3 Future developments

After the third and final pilot market in November a meeting was held with the producers and the organisers in attendance. The purpose of the meeting was to review what the project had achieved and to discuss how the markets could continue and begin to think about becoming self sustaining. The funding had effectively ended with the third market and stallholders would have to begin to consider how they would organise themselves. They agreed on the need to work together and to form some sort of association to facilitate this. A small group of producers and some of the original organisers expressed an interest in forming a working group to consider:

- Formation of an association to facilitate producers working together
- Rules and regulations for the Bath Farmers' Market
- The most effective way of covering the operational costs of the market.
- Day to day management of the market.

At the time of going to print for this case study one meeting of the working group had been held and considerable progress was made towards setting up an association. Further information will be available on this process once it is complete.

Appendix 1
Calendar of events and key decisions

DATE	ACTION
Oct, 1996	• Article in journal on American Farmers' Markets - read by B&NES Local Agenda 21 Coordinator
Nov, 1996	• £2000 funding secured from LGMB Label 21 Awards • Funding matched by B&NES LA 21 project fund and an additional £1750 secured from B&NES Economic Development
Nov, 1996 ongoing	• Database of potential producers developed by B&NES LA 21 Coordinator and assistant
Feb, 1997	• Presentation on Farmers' Markets by Harriet Festing to B&NES Councillors and voluntary sector reps
May, week 4	• Farmers' Market Working Group formed from existing Apple Day Working Group - meets every 2 - 3 weeks
June, week 3	• Additional funding agreed from B&NES LA 21 project budget
July, week 1	• Job descriptions developed for two part-time project officers to work from Bath Environment Centre • Jobs advertised in local press
July, week 2	• Interviews for posts of Project Officer and Reporting Officer
July, week 3	• Project officer posts filled
July, week 4	• Initial contacts with regulatory and licensing authorities
Aug, week 1	• Insurance requirements researched • Project officer meets regulatory and licensing authorities • Potential sites visited and assessed
Aug, week 2	• Visits to potential producer participants • Visit more potential market sites in Bath
Aug, week 3	• Liaison with interested producers and assessing produce
Aug, week 4	• Working Group now meeting once a week • Visiting other markets • Site confirmed for the Bath Farmers' Market as Green Park Station • Liaison on refrigeration • Order banner and 'A' board for publicity • Investigating entertainment options
Sept, week 1	• Working group assesses range of produce • More visits to producers by project officers • Press liaison begins • Liquor licensing process begins • Organisation of cooking demonstrations
Sept, week 2	• Visit to other markets by Research officer • Press releases issued for first market • Liaison with local television, radio and press and national radio • Market photographer and video coverage organised
Sept, week 3	• Working Group meet on site to discuss layout • Radio 5 Live interview

	<ul><li>Local BBC TV feature</li><li>Printing and distribution of fliers</li><li>Dispatch of information pack to producers</li><li>Market decorations ordered</li><li>Booking of tables</li><li>Soliciting donations for charity raffle</li></ul>
Sept, week 4	<ul><li>**First pilot Bath Farmers' Market**</li><li>Working Group meeting</li></ul>
Oct, week 1	<ul><li>Talk to Bath Allotments Group</li><li>Recruitment of additional producers for next market</li></ul>
Oct, week 2	<ul><li>Coverage on national Radio 4, 'The Food Programme'</li><li>Dealing with enquires in response to the market</li><li>Press releases issued for second market</li><li>Confirmation of October Market details to producers</li></ul>
Oct, week 3	<ul><li>**Second pilot Bath Farmers' Market with Apple Day theme**</li><li>Firm up the parameters of the Case Study being written by the Reporting officer</li></ul>
Oct, week 4	<ul><li>Continue recruitment of producers</li></ul>
Nov, week 1	<ul><li>Working Group meeting</li></ul>
Nov, week 2	<ul><li>Confirmation of producers for third market</li></ul>
Nov, week 3	<ul><li>**Third pilot Bath Farmers' Market**</li><li>Followed by meeting with producers to discuss plans for turning market over to them for the future</li></ul>

Appendix 2
Job descriptions for project officer

PART-TIME PROJECT OFFICER

Job description

Farmers' markets: Farmers' markets are a very specific type of market, where the producers sell direct to the consumers, cutting out the middle man. Furthermore, the emphasis is on selling goods close to their source of origin. These features benefit the economy and the environment.

Objectives of the post:

*   to set up and run three pilot farmers' markets in Bath;
*   to assess and report on their commercial viability in the long run.

Key activities:

*   plan and organise three farmers' markets, including finding an appropriate location;
*   liaise with local producers to generate interest in the project and encourage their involvement;
*   draw up guidelines for the market in liaison with regulatory bodies, e.g. planning officers
*   recruit and co-ordinate volunteers as required.

Responsible to:

You will be responsible to the Farmers' Market Steering Group, made up of representatives of Bath and North East Somerset Council, Bath Environment Centre, Bath Organic Group and Bath Permaculture and will report to them on a monthly basis.

Hours: 2 days per week (40 days in total)
Pay: On a self-employed basis, at £75 per day
Place of work: Bath Environment Centre
Duration: July – November 1997
Start date: Immediately

Supported by Bath and North East Somerset Council

PART-TIME REPORTING OFFICER

Job description

Farmers' markets: Farmers' markets are a very specific type of market, where the producers sell direct to the consumers, cutting out the middle man. Furthermore, the emphasis is on selling goods close to their source of origin. These features benefit the economy and the environment.

Objectives of the post:

- to monitor and report on the progress of the project;
- to produce a final report on the project.

Key activities:

- liaise with the Farmers' Market Project Officer in order to monitor progress;
- establish appropriate mechanisms for monitoring the project;
- agree appropriate journals in which to report on the project
- submit articles for publication in journals
- produce a final, in-depth report on the project which, if appropriate, could be used as a good practice guide for farmers' markets.

Responsible to:

You will be responsible to the Farmers' Market Steering Group, made up of representatives of Bath and North East Somerset Council, Bath Environment Centre, Bath Organic Group and Bath Permaculture and will report to them on a monthly basis.

Hours:	1 days per week
Pay:	On a self-employed basis, at £75 per day
Place of work:	Bath Environment Centre
Duration:	July – November 1997
Start date:	Immediately

Supported by Bath and North East Somerset Council

Appendix 3
Guidelines for Bath Farmers' Market

- **General Guidelines for Bath Farmers' Market**
- **Guidelines – Fruit & Vegetables**

General guidelines for Bath Farmers' Market

The Bath Farmers' Market is being established in order to offer local producers of fruit and vegetables, processed foodstuffs and crafts a new retail outlet that enables them to sell direct to the public. The market is planned to be a vibrant and enjoyable place to shop and will give the producers a chance to meet and talk directly to the consumers of the food that they produce.

General

1　Only good quality products and wholesome food should be sold. Produce should be well displayed and presented.
2　The market is only open to the sellers of food and crafts who produce the items themselves. No bought-in produce is allowed to be sold.
3　Only the producer, his/her family or employee is permitted to sell produce. Local growers organisations on this occasion may appoint a representative to sell pooled produce.
4　The market will open at 9.30 a.m. and close at 3.30 p.m. Stalls should not close down or pack up during these hours.
5　Stall holders should label items for sale with their name and address.
6　A fee of £5 per trestle table is chargeable on the day.
7　The allocation of stalls is solely the responsibility of the Market Manager. Stall holders must accept the location of the stall allocated to them.
8　Stall holders should maintain their stall spaces in a clean and sanitary condition and shall remove all boxes, packaging and debris at

the end of the day.

9   Stall holders are advised to post prices of their produce in a clearly visible position.

10   No haranguing or aggressive selling techniques should be employed.

11   All produce should adhere to the rules and regulations of the Food Hygiene (General) Regulations, 1970 and the provisions of the Food Safety Act, 1990 (details available from the Environment Centre, Bath at 24 Milsom Street. Tel no. 01225 460620).

12   There is a No Smoking regulation for those selling foodstuffs.

Guidelines – Fruit & Vegetables

It is intended that the Farmers' Market is a place where people can find good quality and wholesome food at reasonable prices and is not a place for cheap over-ripe reject produce. So only bring the best fruit and vegetables or other produce for sale. There will be competition in the market from both organic and non-organic sellers. Some will have professional experience in selling, so some thought is necessary in the presentation of your stall and selection of your produce.

Packaging

Small items such as soft fruit or leafy items such as winter salads are best pre-packed. Labels should show minimum weight and variety as well as your name and address. Three or 5lb bags of pre-weighed potatoes will help. Polythene bags, nets and punnets can all be used. Some produce is best sold by number such as apples, sweetcorn or onions. Use a maximum of eight items per pack. Produce such as spring onions and radishes can also be bunched. Weight labelling is not required on bunches or countable items.

Pricing

Finding out what the current retail price in your local shop is. Have a special offer on one type of vegetable, but don't try to undercut other sellers. A weighing balance or spring scale that can be hung from a bracket will be required for weighing out produce.

Labelling

Mark the price per unit or weight along with the variety if known on simple display cards. Have your name and farm address well displayed on all labels.

Grading

Do not send low quality or reject fruit or vegetables to market. As there will be some competition from other growers select unusual varieties for sale if possible.

Presentation

Wash soil from vegetables, and leave green stalks on carrots and radishes, ect. Have a small water sprayer to keep the vegetables fresh. Display the produce in rustic baskets or trays. Plastic bowls or bags are not attractive. arrange produce to give a colourful display.

Sampling

Have a tray with vegetables or fruit cut up and speared with cocktail sticks to offer potential buyers.

Appendix 4

local produce for local people
at the

FARMERS' MARKET
BATH

Green Park Station
9.30 a.m. until 3.30 p.m.
Saturday
27 September • 18 October • 15 November

Coverage by the
BBC
Food
Programme

Quality • Freshness • Locally produced • Organic • Free-range • Wholefood
• Live Entertainment Fun & Festivities •

---
local produce on sale ...

Free-range Pork, Sausages, Chicken, & Eggs
Smoked foods,Game & Home baking
Traditional Jersey Clotted Cream
Organic & Speciality Cheeses
Range of locally produced Honey & associated products
British Apples, apple Juice & Cider
OrganicWines, Fruit wines & Mead
Range of Chutneys,Jams, Jellies, Mustards & Marmalades
Breads, Cakes & Savouries
Organic & locally produced Fruit & Vegetables
Cut Flowers
Culinary & Medicinal Herbs
Unusual garden & greenhouse Plants
Fruit Trees, Hedging & Wild flower plants
Crafts

A Case for Farmers' Markets

Farmers have bartered and sold goods as far back in history as agriculture itself, so the concept of a Farmers' Market is not new. However Farmers' Markets are very different in nature to the kind of street markets which are familiar in Britain. They are based on a type of market which has become very popular in the United States.

Farmers' Markets help local producers to sell their goods near their source of origin, creating benefits for producers and the local community. Local, small-scale producers have an outlet for their wares which brings them steady cash flow, flexibility, direct customer feedback and reduced packaging and transport costs. Shoppers gain access to competitively priced, fresh local produce which has been grown, bred, caught, pickled, brewed or baked locally by the vendors themselves.

Farmers' Markets help regeneration of urban and rural areas, and develop goodwill between urban and rural communities. They revitalise spaces such as car parks to provide a vibrant and informal gathering place where friends meet and acquaintances are made.

Some of the more successful Farmers' Markets have covered pavilions, entertainment and hot food. There is an emphasis on quality produce and an upbeat atmosphere. Farmers' Markets make shopping a sociable and enjoyable experience. They benefit the local economy and other shops nearby benefit too, from the spin-off of people attracted to the area by the market. The environment also benefits from Farmers' Markets, because they support local and organic food production and encourage traditional methods of agriculture rather than intensive methods which rely on the use of herbicides and pesticides. Because the goods on sale are produced locally, their transit to the market does not contribute to the environmental damage associated with long distance transportation, and over-packaging is avoided.

Farmers' Markets are good for shoppers, producers, the local economy, street vitality *and* the environment.Show your support - shop at a Farmers' Market and enjoy!
Organised by Bath & North East Somerset Council and the Environment Centre, Bath.

Appendix 5
Press pack

• **News release**
• **Farmers' Market information sheet**
• **Quotations from stallholders and shoppers**

(1) NEWS RELEASE

NEWS RELEASE ... NEWS RELEASE ...

30 October 1997

Farmers' Market comes again to Bath

More 'fruits' of the region are being prepared for the third in a series of pilot Farmers' Markets in Bath this autumn. At Green Park Station on Saturday, 15 November shoppers will be able to taste and buy a range of local produce directly from the producers themselves.

As well as more unusual varieties of vegetables such as Swiss chard and Pink Fir Apples, locally made speciality cheeses, smoked meats, honey, cut flowers, home baking, free range eggs, fruit, wine and cider will be on sale.

Bath Organic Group, who had a stall at the first market in September said, "It's been fantastic! We were selling before we'd unpacked. A lot of people have been asking questions about organic growing. There's a lot of interest and enthusiasm about organic growing in general." One vegetable grower had to rush home to harvest more supplies because he'd been "cleaned out" by mid-morning.

At the market shoppers will have a chance to talk directly to producers. Hugh Tripp, a local organic fruit wine producer from Somerset said, "People have been interested, and a lot of people have bought too. There are not many markets that are suitable for this kind of thing, but this is an exception — it's a very good concept. I've sold a lot of mead and gooseberry wine. Other fruit wines have been very popular — they're all produced locally and people can rest assured that there are no nasty chemicals."

Access to wholesome, locally produced and freshly made, picked, baked or brewed produce at a fair price is proving to be attractive to people — and a festive atmosphere, with musicians, jugglers, puppet theatre and wonderful aromas from a char grill makes shopping an even more enjoyable experience. Derry Watkins of Special Plants, Cold Ashton had a stall in September, and commented, "It's fun to be here. It's like being on holiday — with people laughing and talking to each other."

When a Farmers' Market comes to town other traders benefit from the number of people attracted to the area. A regular vendor at Green Park Station was clearly delighted. She said, "We are doing incredibly well today compared to last week because this is bringing in lots more people. Because of the Farmers' Market there's been a big difference in our takings. It's wonderful and we love it and we hope it happens a lot more often!"

Tony Cox of Mumfords Vineyard in Batheaston said, "It's been busy all day long. The atmosphere's good and the range and quality of produce is superb. If more and more people get to know about it, a Farmers' Market should grow in local importance."

The producers themselves welcome the Farmers' Market as a potential new retail outlet. Graham Padfield, a cheesemaker from Kelston, enjoyed showing customers how his cheese is made, and was able to tell them which local shops stocked his produce. "We don't supply supermarkets", he said, "because we don't make that much — we would have to be ten times bigger." Lower overheads are especially helpful to the small scale producer. They get a better return and are still able to sell at competitive prices because they don't have to pay a 'middleman' or need extra packaging and petrol to get to the market. This has to be good for the environment too, in terms of reducing the pollution and consumption of fossil fuels associated with long distance transportation, and rubbish to be disposed of in the ground as landfill.

The idea of Farmers' Markets has come from the USA, where the Green Markets in New York have become so popular over the last decade that there are now over 2,400 Farmers' Markets established across the

States, with average gross sales of £125,000 per market per year.

If the pilots — a partnership initiative of Bath & North East Somerset Council and The Bath Environment Centre — prove to be viable in Bath, this could be the start of a permanent Farmers' Market for the city and the region — and a way of encouraging local, sustainable food production and consumption, in line with a Local Agenda 21 for the region.

Since BBC Radio 4 featured the Bath Farmers' Market project in 'The Food Programme' in September, this office has received a tremendous amount of interest from local authorities and other organisations all over Britain, wanting to set up Farmers' Markets in their regions. So far, enquiries have come from East Riding, Horsham, Newcastle, Oxfordshire, Leeds, Shrewsbury, Cambridge, Coventry, Barnstaple, Gloucestershire, Essex, Norwich, Jersey, Derbyshire, Matlock, Gwynedd, Shaftesbury, Maidstone, North Lincolnshire, Cheshire, Edinburgh, Cumbria, Kent, Exeter, Pembrokeshire, Harrow, High Wycombe, Sussex and some London boroughs.

Our working group is presently preparing a case study and report which should be available towards the end of November. Anyone who is interested in the report, or would like to receive a copy should contact either Deborah Morris (01225 477662) or Patricia Tutt (01225 477653) at this office.

ENDS

Contacts: Deborah Morris, Assistant Local Agenda 21 Co-ordinator
             Bath & North East Somerset Council
             daytime (01225) 477662

             Patricia Tutt, Local Agenda 21 Co-ordinator
             Bath & North East Somerset Council
             daytime (01225) 477653

             Sarah May, Farmers' Market Project Officer
             The Environment Centre, Bath
             daytime (01225) 460620 (Tuesdays only)
             evening (01225) 891831

Photo opportunities

Producers preparing, harvesting, etc (please telephone direct to arrange a mutually convenient time)

Sue Elcock, Special Plants, Cold Ashton 01225 891250 (unusual garden plants)

Hugh Tripp, Avalon Vineyards, East Pennard, Shepton Mallet 01749 860393 (organic fruit wines and mead)

Graham Padfield, Bath Soft Cheese, Park Farm, Kelston 01225 424139 (cheeses)

Background Notes on Local Agenda 21

Agenda 21 emerged from the United Nations' Earth Summit in Rio in 1992 as a response to growing international alarm about global environmental degradation and threats. It is an international agreement which calls for better quality of human life across the globe, and presents a world-wide agenda for the 21st century. Agenda 21 is a process which seeks to enable all of the world's peoples to meet their basic needs without exceeding the carrying capacity of the Earth's life support systems, or compromising the ability of future generations to meet their needs.

Local Agenda 21 focuses on communities and individuals to bring about sustainable patterns of development at a local level. It is about the quality of life we experience in our familiar environment, and also the far-reaching effects of our lifestyles on other parts of the world.

In relation to Local Agenda 21, a Farmers' Market addresses social, economic and environmental issues. Please see more detailed notes on Farmers' Markets, attached.

(2) FARMERS' MARKETS INFORMATION SHEET

What is a farmers' market?

The concept of farmers' markets is obviously not a new one. Farmers have bartered and sold goods as far back in history as agriculture itself. The term 'farmers' market' is used here in a very specific way. It is based on the model of a type of market currently on the increase in the USA and which is very different in nature to the kind of street markets which have become familiar in Britain.

The main emphasis of these markets is that they help local producers, processors and manufacturers to sell their goods near their source of origin, creating benefits to them and to the local community. One third of all stallholders in the US use these markets as their sole marketing outlet, and 2/3 of the markets are certified or regulated, the idea being that the vendors have grown, bred, caught pickled, brewed, or baked the goods themselves.

The markets give an advantage to the producer over selling to a middleman, and they benefit the local economy. In addition they create many social and health opportunities. Last but not least they help the environmental sustainability of the local area by encouraging organic production, reducing transportation miles, pollution, packaging and waste and promoting associated recycling activities.

Farmers' markets place an emphasis on added value, quality and freshness. They often have associated music and festival events, sometimes with a seasonal theme. They aim for an atmosphere which is vibrant, upbeat and fun, helping to revitalise urban centres and to make shopping a sociable and enjoyable experience.

What is the benefit to the producer?

In the USA farmers' markets play a vital role in enabling small and medium sized growers to gain direct access to consumers. Over 20,000 farmers sell through them. It is estimated that the 'Greenmarkets' in New York City generate more than $20 million in sales to regional growers. One million consumers in America visit the markets every week. Benefits are obtained because;

- Direct selling (rather than through wholesalers or supermarkets) allows for premium prices.
- Cash flow is improved and steadier.
- Farmers and processors can get direct customer feedback allowing them to improve their service and product development.
- The need for transportation and packaging is reduced, saving on costs.
- There is less wastage from outgrades e.g. fruit and vegetables not uniform enough in size, colour, shape etc. to be sold to a supermarket.
- Small scale producers who do not achieve a great enough quantity for a supermarket contract can have an outlet for their goods.

- Ethnic minorities, women and small scale businesses including part-time farmers can gain market access and support.
- Farmers and producers working isolation get more job satisfaction from social contact and interaction with their customers.
- Local growers and processors do not have to compete with larger companies from outside the area. The certification ensures that only local businesses can sell.

FARMERS MARKETS — A MODEL FOR SUSTAINABLE DEVELOPMENT

What are the social, economic and environmental benefits?

Social

Farmers' markets help;
- Revitalise village, town and city centres
- Provide a social meeting point
- Encourage interaction of people from all walks of life.
- Promote goodwill and understanding between rural and urban populations.
- Allow people working in isolated situations to meet their customers and other producers
- Provide a health diet for local people through access to fresher produce.
- Provide cheaper good quality food which is especially important for people on low incomes
- Women and others with special commitments who need greater flexibility with working hours.
- Provide support for music, drama and festive events.
- Attract media and publicity attention to rural development issues.
- Convey an educational awareness message to the public about where and how their food is produced.

Economic

Farmers' markets are;
- An employment provider and can aid adjacent retailers and other

economic development.

- Able to attract business at times and in places where trading may not normally take place, with spin off benefits to other traders.
- A mechanism to encourage agricultural diversification, thus creating a more stable economy.
- A way of establishing links with the farming community and agencies, towards partnership working.
- A way of encouraging the consumer to buy local produce and support local business.
- A way to provide ethical investment opportunities.
- A method of encourage Local Exchange Trading Systems (LETS)

Environmental

Farmers' markets can;
- Be a useful mechanism for implementing Local Agenda 21.
- Reduce the transportation of goods, so using less 'food miles' and less fossil fuels.
- Reduce vehicle generated air pollution and noise.
- Reduce wastage from outgrades.
- Encourage more organic production so less pesticide and herbicide use.
- Benefit wildlife by less destruction of their habitat and food sources due to less intensive farming practices.
- Encourage farm diversification which usually helps biodiversity.
- Help raise awareness about sustainable development and the links between society, the economy and the environment.

(3) QUOTATIONS FROM STALLHOLDERS AND SHOPPERS AT THE FARMERS' MARKET ON SATURDAY, 27 SEPTEMBER 1997

"The Farmers' Market has exceeded all our expectations. It's been very busy and we've sold a lot of stuff." Vegetable grower

"Fantastic! We were selling before we unpacked the stuff this morning." Bath Organic Growers

"My husband has gone back for more supplies because we've been cleaned out". Vegetable grower

"Everyone seems really pleased to have this available to them. Lots of people have asked where we are." Vegetable grower

"We've sold out of yellow tomatoes, spinach and ruby chard — as fresh as it can be."

"Things have gone as well as expected. There's been a lot of enthusiasm and people asking questions about organic growing in general. There's a lot of interest in organic growing." Organic grower

"I came along to buy organic fruit and vegetables — and to see if the market is working. And it is — it's brilliant!" Councillor Roger Symonds

"It's such a lovely atmosphere. It's fun to be here. much busier than I had expected. It's like being on holiday, with people laughing and talking to each other. It feels so open and cheerful. I recently went to a Farmers' Market in America, and I'm very glad I did." Derry Watkins of Special Plants, Cold Ashton (she sells at major flower shows)

"This is fantastic! It's brilliant!" An American living in Bath

"This is good because we are talking to people — to the customer. I have been amazed by how much people are prepared to buy. It will be good for shop keepers nearby aswell. We do not supply supermarkets because we do not make that much — we would have to be 10 times bigger. The market adds interest to the area. We will definitely be here next time." Graham Padfield, Bath Soft Cheese, Kelston

"People have been interersted and a lot of people have bought too. It's good to know from experience what's going to be popular. There are not many markets that are suitable for this kind of thing, but this one is an exception — it's a very good concept. I've sold a lot of mead and gooseberry wine. Other fruit wines have been very popular — they're all organically produced in Somerset, and people can rest assured that there are no nasty chemicals." Hugh Tripp, Avalon Vineyards, Shepton Mallet

"It's been busy all day long. The atmosphere's good, the range of produce excellent — with superb organic, locally grown vegetables, fruit, flowers, dairy produce and meat. People have been able to sample the full range of my wine, and have taken literature and expressed interest in coming to see us. People are suggesting this event might happen more frequently. If more and more people get to know about it, the Farmers' Market should grow in local importance." Tony Cox, Mumford's

Vineyard, Batheaston

"We are doing incredibly well today, compared to last week because this is bringing in lots more people. We have a regular stall up there by the shop. We have done an awful lot better because people are coming for the Farmers' Market rather than just parking and going into Sainsbury's. There has been a big difference in our takings. It's wonderful and we love it and we hope it happens a lot more often." Regular stall-holder

"It's been fantastic. I think it's a brilliant idea. It's done the regular market some good — it's livened up the whole place." Shoppers

Appendix 6
Questionnaire to Farmers' Market stallholders

This project is breaking ground in new ways to encourage local food production. As part of the project we are collecting and disseminating information on good practice. Your assistance with this is very much appreciated and will help us in promoting Farmers' Markets throughout the U.K.

Name _____

Address _____

_____

Post Code _____ Telephone _____

Produce for sale

1. How long have you been producing these goods? _____

2. Where do you currently sell your produce? *(please indicate % sales of each outlet where applicable)*

[ ] No current sales	[%] Local shops
[%] Wholesaler	[%] Other street market
[%] Farm shop	[%] Other *(please specify below)*

   Other _____

3. How many days each weeek are you involved in selling your produce? _____

4. What is the minimum daily turnover you would need to attend a Farmers' Market? £ _____

5. If the Farmers' Market is popular and becomes a regular market;

   which hours of the day should the market operate? *From* _____ *a.m.* *To* _____ *p.m.*

   which day of the week should the market operate? _____

   how many days each month should the market operate? _____

6. How much land do you have? _____

7. How many employees do you have? *(please enter number in box(es) as appropriate)*

   [ ] paid family members   [ ] unpaid family and friends   [ ] paid non-family

8. Will you supply a Farmers' Market all year round? *(please tick a box)* ☐ Yes ☐ No

    If not please ring which months you could   J   F   M   A   M   J   J   A   S   O   N   D

9. What was your turnover on 15th November?   _____

10. Would you in future alter your production plan to supply a regular Farmers' Market? ☐ Yes ☐ No
    (please tick a box)

11. Would you attend other Farmers Markets in the region? *(please tick a box)* ☐ Yes ☐ No

    If yes how far would you travel?   _____ miles

12. Why have you decided to participate in the Bath Farmers' Market? *(please tick box(es) as appropriate)*

    ☐ Chance to start new business

    ☐ Chance to expand sales

    ☐ Opportunity to meet customers and get feedback

    ☐ Chance to test new lines

    ☐ Chance to sell excess produce

    ☐ Want to encourage direct selling initiatives

    ☐ Other (please specify) _____

Future direction of Farmers Markets

12. Would you like the Farmers' Market to be? *(please tick boxes as appropriate)*

    ☐ A regular weekly market

    ☐ A regular annual or twice a year festival of local produce

    ☐ To allow both local and bought-in produce to be sold

    ☐ A market where only locally produced food is sold

13. Would you be interested in becoming involved in the organisation of Farmers' Markets? *(please tick a box)*

    ☐ Yes   ☐ No

14. Would you be interested in selling at Farmers' Markets in any other towns or venues? *(please tick a box)*

    ☐ Yes   ☐ No

Appendix 7
Telephone questions for stallholders

Note: Please return your questionnaire if you have not aleady done so.

Name of Stallholder							

1. What was your turnover on 29 September?								
1. What was your turnover on 18 October?								

2. How does this compare with your other outlets?

better								
the same								
worse								

3. Will you be attending the Farmers' Market on 15 November?

yes								
no								
if yes, how many tables will you need?								

4. Will you be interested in attending the Farmers' Market on 13 December, given it will be run on a commercial basis with stall charges @ £35 - £45

yes								
no								
if yes, how many tables will you need?								
if no, what is a reasonable charge for a stall?								

5. What problems did you find on the day?

parking								
lack of stall space								
length of day								
competition								
insurance								
insufficient stock								
other. Please specify:								

6. Do you have any suggestions for improvement?

better advertisements								
more press coverage								
better parking								
longer/shorter opening hours								
alternative site								
more space								
more/fewer stalls								
more/less entertainment								

Appendix 8
Customer survey results

CUSTOMER SURVEY RESULTS

1. Age of customers

0-20 yrs	4%
21-40 yrs	40%
41+ yrs	55%
male	33%
female	67%

notes: Many couples shopping as it was a Saturday.

2. How did you hear about this market?

Advert in paper	26%
Radio/TV	36%
Posters	20%
Word of mouth	26%
Passer-by	6%

Other: Environment centre (5), organic group circular (3), dentist/doctor surgery, newspaper article were mentioned once each

3. What have you bought ?

Fruit and vegetables	74%
Dairy produce	30%
Meat Products	26%
Baked goods	28%
other processed goods	24%
Craftwork	7%

Notes: There is a need to be more imaginative with craftwork.

4. Where do you normally buy these products?

Supermarket	65%
Corner shop	15%
Greengrocer	27%
General Grocer	8%
Grow own	8%
Farm Shop	11%
Guildhall Market	5%
organic/health shop	5%

Other: Butcher(7), Organic farm or box scheme(2),

Notes: Interesting diversity of answers especially as people were so close to Sainsburys and many were doing their weekly shop there.

5.   How much have you spent

less than £3	24%
£3-10	37%
£10-20	31%
£20+	7%

6.   Why did you buy from the FM?

It was cheap	9%
It was good quality	45%
It was directly from the producer	38%
It was freshly made/harvested	47%
It was not available elsewhere	15%
I like to support local business	37%
Because it was organic	14%

Other: Like the social atmosphere (6), convenient (2),
Notes: Confirms the idea that it should be exclusively for producers only with 38% giving this as a reason and 37% also for supporting local business.

7.   Why didn't you buy other products?

Things were expensive	11%
There was little choice	4%
There was no guarantee of quality	2%
Looking for a specific product	19%
Prefer the convenience of the supermarket	4%
No need already bought	20%
Goods too heavy to transport home	8%

Other: grow own (6), no money (12), too crowded (8), too busy (4), food will go off before get home (6)

8.   What other goods would you like to buy?
Nothing more needed (24), more meat (17), more bread (16), more vegetables (15),
more baked goods (11), more cheese,dairy products, eggs, mushrooms (all 7)

8.   How often should the market operate?

Once a week	48%
once a fortnight	29%

once a month	21%
2 or 3 times/year	2%

9.   How far have you travelled to get here?

0-1 mile	29%
2-3 miles	28%
3-10 miles	18%
10+ miles	26%

10.   Is this a good time to hold a FM?

Yes	98%
No	2%

11.   Would you be interested in selling at the market yourself?

Yes	19%
No	76%
Perhaps	4%